# Second Edition
# Cambridge Primary Path 3

**Grammar and Writing Workbook**

Catherine Zgouras

# Contents

| Unit | Grammar | Learn to Write | Writing |
|---|---|---|---|
| 1 What makes your community special? page 3 | Could/couldn't for Ability with when <br><br> Tense Review | Titles in Names | A Letter |
| 2 What is food for? page 13 | Present Progressive with Future Meaning <br><br> Should/shouldn't, must/mustn't | Before and after + Noun | An Invitation |
| 3 Why do we need to take care of nature? page 23 | Past Progressive <br><br> Interrupted Past | Possessive Nouns | A Brochure |

**Unit 1–3 Review page 93**

| Unit | Grammar | Learn to Write | Writing |
|---|---|---|---|
| 4 What is art? page 33 | Comparative and Superlative Adjectives <br> Comparative and Superlative Adverbs | Pronouns | A Diary Entry |
| 5 Why do we travel? page 43 | Comparatives <br> Gerunds as Subjects and Objects | Because | A Travel Blog |
| 6 Why do we play sports? page 53 | Zero Conditional <br><br> Have to | Sequence Adverbs | Instructions |

**Unit 4–6 Review page 94**

| Unit | Grammar | Learn to Write | Writing |
|---|---|---|---|
| 7 How can we explore the past? page 63 | May and might <br><br> Give, send, take, bring, show | Capitalization | A News Report |
| 8 How important is electricity? page 73 | Will <br><br> Future Plans with going to | Time Words | An Advertisement |
| 9 Why do we have music? page 83 | Making Promises or Offers with will <br><br> Past Progressive Parallel Actions with while | Conjunctions | A Music Shape Poem |

**Unit 7–9 Review page 95**

# 1 What makes your community special?

**Grammar:** could/couldn't for Ability with when

## Interesting People ...

My name's Evan, and I live in small town with lots of interesting people. Let's meet some of them.

This is Sally. She's a cook. When she was 17, she couldn't cook, so she went to school to learn. It was far away, but that was OK. She could drive.

This is Tim. He owns a bike store. When he was 19, he could fix bikes. He could ride bikes fast, too, and he won a lot of competitions. However, he wasn't very good with cars. He couldn't fix them. He still can't!

My neighbor Julie is very smart. When she was four, she could read and write. She couldn't draw, though.

This is me and my best friend, Scott. We love sports. When we were five, we could ride our bikes, but we couldn't rollerblade. Now we can do both.

**1** Read the poster. Why are the people interesting?

**2** Read again. Complete the sentences.

a When Sally was 17, she _couldn't_ cook, but she _____ drive.

b When Tim was 19, he _____ fix a car, but he _____ fix bikes.

c Julie _____ read and write when she was four.

d When Evan and Scott were five, they _____ ride bikes, but they _____ rollerblade.

3

## Grammar: could/couldn't for Ability with when

We use *could* and *couldn't* to talk about ability in the past.

**When** Tony was four, he **couldn't** skateboard.
**When** Tony was eight, he **could** rollerblade very well.

We can use short answers to answer *yes/no* questions.

**Could** Jenny ride a bike when she was three?    **No**, she **couldn't**.
**Could** she swim?                                **Yes**, she **could**.

**Remember**
We use the base form of the verb after *could* and *couldn't*.

**3) Look and read. Choose the correct words.**

a She **could** / (**couldn't**) play soccer when she was six.

b He **could** / **couldn't** skateboard when he was young.

c When they were six, they **could** / **couldn't** play basketball.

d When Dina was five, she **could** / **couldn't** rollerblade.

e When Pete was young, he **could** / **couldn't** ride a bike.

**4) Look at the table and complete the paragraph with *could* and *couldn't*.**

|  | Sarah | Dan |
|---|---|---|
| Draw | ✓ | ✗ |
| Write | ✗ | ✓ |
| Read a Book | ✗ | ✓ |
| Speak English | ✓ | ✗ |

Sarah is my younger sister. When she was four, she 1 ____could____ draw, but she 2 _____ write. She 3 _____ read a book, but she 4 _____ speak English.

Dan is my best friend. When he was four, he 5 _____ draw, but he 6 _____ read and write. He 7 _____ speak English.

5) **Read and complete the questions. Then, match to the answers.**

swim  ~~run~~  cook  rollerblade  read

1  Could Sam _____run_____ fast when he was four?  [a]
2  Could you _____ dinner when you were six?  [ ]
3  Could Sally _____ a book when she was six?  [ ]
4  Could Billy and Penny _____ when they were seven?  [ ]
5  Could we _____ when we were babies?  [ ]

a  Yes, he could.   c  Yes, they could.   e  No, we couldn't.
b  No, she couldn't.   d  No, I couldn't.

6) **Look. Answer the questions.**

a  Could Joe rollerblade? __No, he couldn't__.
b  Could Tanya ride a bike? _____.
c  Could they play tennis? _____.
d  Could they jump rope? _____.
e  Could he play basketball? _____.
f  Could the baby girl walk? _____.

7) **Complete the sentences about you.**

a  When I was four, I could _____,
   but I couldn't _____.

b  When I was _____,
   _____.

c  Now I can _____,
   but I can't _____.

**Grammar:** Tense Review

### My Town: Patras—Old and New

Patras is an ancient city in southern Greece.

Twenty years ago, Patras was very different. There weren't any parks, and people didn't have anywhere to go for a walk. People didn't ride bikes, and children stayed indoors. The ocean was very dirty. People had to go far from town when they wanted to go to the beach.

Today, there is a big park where I ride my bike. People walk in the park and have picnics there, too. The ocean isn't dirty anymore. In the summer, my friends and I always swim in the ocean near the center of town. We don't have to travel to beaches far away.

I'm at the park now and I'm waiting for my friends. Many people from our town are here. We are getting ready to ride our bikes through the park and down to the beach.

👍 300   👎        REPLY

Show comments (56) ⌄

**1** Read the blog. How has the city changed?

**2** Read the sentences. Write *past*, *present*, or *right now*.

  a  People didn't ride bikes, and children played indoors. _____

  b  We are getting ready to ride our bikes. _____

  c  People walk in the park and have picnics, too. _____

**Grammar: Tense Review**

We use the present simple to talk about events that happen every day, things in general, or facts.

We use the present progressive to talk about actions happening right now.

We use the past simple to talk about events that happened yesterday, last week, last year, or a long time ago.

|  | Affirmative | Negative | Questions | Short answers |
|---|---|---|---|---|
| Present Simple | We listen to music. It works. | They don't watch TV. He doesn't play soccer. | Do you ride a bike? Does she like tennis? | Yes, I do. No, I don't. Yes, she does. No, she doesn't. |
| Present Progressive | I am swimming in the ocean. She is sitting in the park. You are playing tennis. | I'm not walking home. He isn't doing his homework. They aren't waiting for you. | Am I watching the show? Is he going to the park? Are we reading a book? | Yes, I am. No, I'm not. Yes, he is. No, he isn't. Yes, we are. No, we aren't. |
| Past Simple | They visited their cousins. | I didn't talk to him. | Did he ask a question? | Yes, he did. No, he didn't. |

**3** Read the sentences and underline the verbs. Then, match to the correct tense.

1. Joe <u>came</u> home early last night. **c**
2. I don't watch TV every day. ☐
3. Paul is walking the dog now. ☐
4. Does Tony study in the evenings? ☐

   a present simple
   b present progressive
   c past simple

**Spelling Rule**

With many verbs, we form the past simple by adding -ed. These are called *regular verbs*.

play ⟶ played

The past simple of irregular verbs doesn't have the + -ed ending.

swim ⟶ swam
go ⟶ went
have ⟶ had

**4** Read and choose the correct words.

a We always **are having / (have)** a big breakfast on Sunday.
b **Do you write / Are you writing** a letter at the moment?
c Laura **doesn't see / didn't see** her friends last weekend.
d Ben and Tom **came / come** to soccer practice early yesterday.

## 5) Look at the pictures. Then, complete the sentences.

a Tara _____visited_____ her grandmother last week. (visit)

b Jo and his family _____ to the beach now. (drive)

c The dog _____ the cat at the moment. (not chase)

d They usually _____ a kite in the park. (fly)

e Sarah _____ computer games last night. (not play)

## 6) Rewrite the sentences in the affirmative, negative, or question form.

a We have piano lessons every Tuesday.
✗ We don't have piano lessons every Tuesday.

b Is Dad working now?
✔ _____

c They saw the new movie last week.
✗ _____

d Does Mary swim in the ocean?
✗ _____

e They played tennis yesterday.
? _____

f John walks to school every morning.
? _____

## 7) Complete the sentences about you.

a I always _____.

b At the moment, _____.

c Yesterday, _____.

## Improve Your Writing: Titles in Names

### Titles in Names

We use titles in names when we talk to adults that we don't know well or to be polite.

We use *Mr.* for a man.

We can use *Miss* for a young woman who is not married.

We can use *Mrs.* for a woman who is married.

We can use *Ms.* for any woman.

 This is **Mr**. Jones.

 This is **Miss** Smith.

 This is **Mrs**. Taylor.

 This is **Ms**. Cook.

**1** Look and write. You can use more than one title.

> Mr.   Miss   Mrs.   Ms.

a ____Mr.____ Banks

b _____ Thompson

c _____ Sarah Russel

d _____ and _____ Hogan

e _____ Daniels

**2** Read and choose the correct word.

a My teacher isn't married. Her name is **Mrs.** / **Miss** Patty Dunn.

b What's his name? It's **Mrs.** / **Mr.** Rashid.

c Is **Mrs.** / **Miss** Sommers your grandmother?

d **Ms.** / **Mr.** Brown is our music teacher. She's nice.

e My sister got married last week. Her new name is **Miss** / **Mrs.** West.

**Writing: A Letter**

**1 READ** Read the letter. Who is Tom writing about?

May 25
Botany Elementary School
15 King Street, Mascot

Dear Mrs. Bray,

I want to nominate Mr. Tony Anders for the Best Teacher award. He's our science teacher this year, and he always makes the classes interesting.

He's a great teacher because he explains everything, and we do a lot of experiments with him in class. He always gives us ideas about how to make our environment a better place to live in.

Best of all, Mr. Anders always has time for his students after class or after school and talks to us about many different things.

Best wishes,
Tom Zachs

**2 EXPLORE** Read and write *Yes* or *No*.

In a letter, you …

a  write the date. — Yes

b  write your friend's address. — ____

c  start with your name. — ____

d  start with *Dear* and (sometimes) a title. — ____

e  end with the date. — ____

f  write *Best wishes* or similar at the beginning. — ____

**3  PLAN**  Think about who you would nominate as Best Teacher and why. Then, complete the graphic organizer.

Who you will nominate?
_____

Why you will nominate them?

| | | |
|---|---|---|

**4  WRITE**  Write a letter to your school principal to nominate a teacher for a Best Teacher award. Use your ideas from the graphic organizer.

_____
_____
_____
_____
_____
_____
_____
_____
_____
_____

**CHECK**

**Did you ...**  • write the date? ☐    • write the correct titles? ☐
  • write the correct address? ☐    • write an ending? ☐

# Practice Your Exam Skills

Katy is visiting her grandmother. Katy is asking her grandma questions about her life. What does her grandma say?

Read the conversation and choose the best answers. Write a letter (a–h) for each answer. You do not need to use all of the letters.

**Example**  Katy – Grandma, could you ride a bike when you were young?

Grandma – ____e____

1  Katy – What else could you do? Could you swim?

Grandma – _____

2  Katy – Really? I love the ocean. Did you play with your friends?

Grandma – _____

3  Katy – What kind of games did you play? Did you play computer games?

Grandma – _____

4  Katy – That's interesting. What about now? Do you go shopping every day?

Grandma – _____

5  Katy – What about your evenings? Do you always watch TV in the evenings?

Grandma – _____

a  Yes, I did. We played in the streets or the park.
b  No, I don't. I sometimes go shopping on the weekend.
c  No, I couldn't. I didn't like the ocean.
d  Yes, I do. I like watching TV.
e  Yes, I could. I rode my bike to school every day.
f  No, I didn't. We didn't have computers. We played board games.
g  I'm swimming in the ocean.
h  Because we are having a nice time.

12

# 2 What is food for?

**Grammar:** Present Progressive with Future Meaning

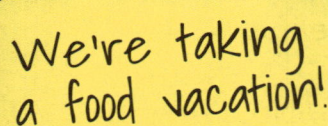
We're taking a food vacation!

On Monday, I am going to a noodle festival. I love ramen noodles and seaweed in a special meat soup. It's delicious and very healthy. On Monday evening, we are taking part in a cooking competition. I can't wait. – Daiki, Japan

Next weekend, there's a chocolate festival in my town. My brother is selling his chocolate tarts. They're delicious! On Saturday, we are watching a chocolate fashion show. The models wear chocolate dresses! We aren't going to the festival on Sunday. We are driving back home.
– Mary, United States

My parents are taking me to a chestnut festival this weekend. It's my first time. On Saturday night, we are having a big dinner in the town square. Mom and I are making chestnut jam for everybody.
– Paolo, Italy

Are you going to a food festival in your area? Write and tell us about it!

**1** Read the blog and match the person to the food.

1 Daiki    2 Mary    3 Paolo

 a   b   c

chestnuts    chocolate    noodles

**2** Read the blog again and match.

| a | Daiki | aren't making | to a cooking competition. |
| b | Mary's brother | is taking | a big dinner in the town square. |
| c | The models | are having | chocolate tarts. |
| d | Paolo and his mom | isn't going | part in a competition. |
| e | Paolo | is selling | chocolate clothes. |

13

**Grammar: Present Progressive with Future Meaning**

We use the present progressive to talk about future plans.

**I am making dinner with my Dad this weekend.**

We often use a time phrase to say when something is happening.

We form the present progressive with *am/is/are/'m not/isn't/aren't* and a verb + *ing*.

| Affirmative | Questions | Short answers |
| --- | --- | --- |
| I am going to Japan this weekend. | Am I having a party? | Yes, you are. / No, you aren't. |
| My brother is presenting his project on Friday. | Is the girl visiting her grandparents tomorrow? | Yes, he/she/it is. No, he/she/it isn't. |
| Mom and I are making chestnut jam tonight. | Are you taking part in any food festivals? | Yes, I am. / No, I'm not. Yes, we/you/they are. No, we/you/they aren't. |

**Spelling Rule**

say ⟶ +ing ⟶ play**ing**
dance ⟶ +ing ⟶ danc**ing**
tie ⟶ +ing ⟶ ty**ing**
stop ⟶ +ing ⟶ stopp**ing**

**3** Read and circle the correct word.

a She **isn't** / aren't going on vacation this summer.
b **Is** / **Are** the boys playing soccer next week?
c I **am** / **is** working on my project this weekend.
d John and I **aren't** / **am not** taking a test on Wednesday.

**4** Unscramble the sentences.

a My twin cousins / on Sunday / are having / a birthday party

My twin cousins are having a birthday party on Sunday.

b to work / isn't going / Dad / tomorrow

_____

c I / my parents / this weekend / am helping / with the housework

_____

d he / saving / Is / a new video game / money for

_____

5) **Read and complete the sentences with the present progressive.**

Hi, Jane!

I got some great news this week. We 1 <u>are planning</u> (plan) to go to Europe this summer! First, we 2 _____ (visit) Rome. There's a pizza festival and I 3 _____ (make) my famous cheese and tomato pizza.
Then, we 4 _____ (fly) to France. My brother 5 _____ (meet) his friends from his art school, and they 6 _____ (put) on an art exhibition.
Dad 7 _____ (not/drive) us around Europe because it takes too long.
We 8 _____ (travel) by train. What are you doing this summer?
Write soon!
Tony

SEND

6) **Look and write sentences. Write when they are doing the activity.**

a — tomorrow
b — Monday morning
c — Friday
d — the weekend
e — next week
f — next month

a  Sara / read / book.
   <u>Sara is reading a book tomorrow.</u>

b  Mrs. Mills / go / to the market.
   _____

c  Tony and Luke / ride bikes.
   _____

d  Dad / not make / dinner. / He / paint the house.
   _____

e  Lucy and Tom / visit / grandparents.
   _____

f  Anna / not play tennis. / She / play soccer.
   _____

7) **Make two sentences about you.**

a  _____ next month.

b  _____ this weekend.

**Grammar:** *should/shouldn't, must/mustn't*

# The Food Doctor
Food expert Dr. Smith answers your questions.

**Q:** My friend feels tired at school. What should he do?
**Carol, 10**

**A:** He should have a good breakfast every morning. Oatmeal and orange juice are a good way to start the day.

**Q:** Do you have any advice on what food to eat when we have exams at school?
**Tom, 10**

**A:** You should eat lots of healthy foods, such as fruits and vegetables. You shouldn't eat too many snacks, and you mustn't eat junk food. You'll feel bad and you'll stop studying. Some chocolate before an exam is fine, but you shouldn't eat too much!

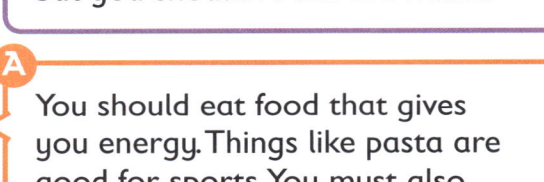

**Q:** I have a soccer tournament on Sunday. What should I eat and drink?
**Penny, 9**

**A:** You should eat food that gives you energy. Things like pasta are good for sports. You must also drink lots of water. It's important that your body gets lots of liquids.

**1 Read the text and match.**

a Carol
b Tom
c Penny

**2 Read again and complete the sentences.**

a He __should__ have a good breakfast every morning.

b You _____ eat too many snacks, and you _____ eat junk food.

c You _____ also drink lots of water.

**Grammar:** *should/shouldn't, must/mustn't*

We use *should* and *shouldn't* to give advice.

**You should go to bed early.**
**You shouldn't go out when you are sick.**

We use *must* and *mustn't* to give strong advice or set a rule. *Must* is stronger than *should*.

**You must tell the teacher.**
**We mustn't steal.**

**3  Read and circle the correct word.**

a  I think you **should** / **must** always try to do your best in school.
b  We **shouldn't** / **mustn't** take things that don't belong to us. It's illegal.
c  We **must** / **should** arrive on time for class. It's the school rules.
d  When there's a hurricane, people **must** / **should** stay indoors, or they could get badly hurt.
e  We **mustn't** / **shouldn't** eat too many snacks because it's bad for our health.
f  Everyone **should** / **must** eat heathy food if they don't want to get sick.

**4  Complete the sentences with *should*, *shouldn't*, *must*, or *mustn't*.**

a  We _____should_____ eat fruit and vegetables every day.
b  People _____ light fires in forests. It's a crime.
c  My advice is that you _____ stay up so late.
d  You _____ be quiet in the library. It's a rule.
e  We _____ get lots of exercise because it's good for us.

**5** Complete the sentences with the correct form of the verbs.

1. Your friend isn't feeling well.
2. You are always tired in the morning.
3. An older woman on the bus has nowhere to sit.
4. You got 50% on a test, but you tell your parents you got 80%.
5. People are leaving their garbage behind on the beach.

a. You should stand up and give her your seat. ____
b. You mustn't lie to your parents. ____
c. They mustn't leave their garbage on the beach. ____
d. He should see a doctor. __1__
e. You should go to bed earlier. ____

**6** Imagine you are going on a camping trip. Make sentences with *should*, *shouldn't*, *must*, or *mustn't*.

a. You __shouldn't put__ too many things in your bag.
b. You _____ to strangers. It's dangerous.
c. You _____ plenty of water.
d. You _____ a fire when it's hot outside. It's illegal.
e. You _____ always _____ near your guide so you don't get lost.

**7** Read and write sentences about yourself.

a. Write one thing you should do at home.
_____

b. Write one thing you shouldn't do in the park.
_____

c. Write one thing you must do when crossing the street.
_____

d. Write one thing you mustn't do in a library.
_____

**Improve Your Writing:** *before* and *after* + Noun

**Before** and **after** + Noun

We use *before* and *after* to explain the order of events.
We use *before* and *after* with a noun.

**Before** dinner, we set the table.
(First, we set the table. Then, we have dinner.)

**After** dinner, we wash the dishes.
(First, we have dinner. Then, we wash the dishes.)

**1** Look and write *before* or *after*.

a  ___Before___  dinner, Mr. Perez reads his newspaper.

b  _____  lunch, she washes her hands.

c  _____  school, he does his homework.

d  _____  bedtime, they put away their toys.

e  _____  the party, the children clean up.

**2** Read and number the events.

a  After the game, I take a shower.

  __1__         __2__

b  Before breakfast, I take the dog for a walk.

  ____          ____

c  After school, we play in the backyard.

  ____          ____

19

# Writing: An Invitation

**1 READ** Read the invitation. What's happening on Tuesday?

To: Students at Johnstone Middle School, 1

From: The Principal 5

Please come to the eighth grade baking competition. 2 It's on Tuesday, July 7, from 5 p.m. to 8 p.m. in the gymnasium. 3 Please bring money to buy cupcakes and drinks. 6 We will be collecting money for charity. There will be a concert after the competition. 4

**2 EXPLORE** Where are these things in the invitation? Read and write the number.

a  who the invitation is to             1
b  who the invitation is from           ___
c  instructions on what to bring        ___
d  when the event is happening          ___
e  what is happening at the event       ___
f  where the event is taking place      ___

**3 PLAN** You're going to organize an event. Use the graphic organizer to help you plan.

- Type of Event: _____
- Place: _____
- Date and Time: _____
- What People Should Bring: _____
- What People Will Do Before: _____
- What People Will Do After: _____

**4 WRITE** Write your invitation. Use the graphic organizer to help you.

_____
_____
_____
_____
_____

**CHECK**

Did you ...
- write the day and date? ☐
- write the place? ☐
- write what you are going to do there? ☐
- write *To* and *From*? ☐
- write the time? ☐
- write what to bring? ☐

**Practice Your Exam Skills**

Read the diary and write the missing words. Write one word on each line.

**Example**   We are ____going____ camping on Sunday for a whole week. It's going to be fun!

1   There's a big swimming _____ where we can go swimming in the morning. We can play lots of sports there, too.

2   We _____ run in the pool area because it's dangerous.

3   My _____ sport is tennis. I love it. I'm going to play every day.

4   The camp has _____ few rules. This is so everyone has a good time and is safe.

5   One rule _____ that we should always be nice to everyone and help each other. That way everyone is happy. I think summer camp will be great!

# 3 Why do we need to take care of nature?

**Grammar:** Past Progressive

Hello. Timmy Tracker here, in Australia. Look at these footprints! Footprints are great. They tell us a lot about what made them. But whose footprints are these? Let's follow them and find out.

I think these footprints were made by a bird. They were also made by a big bird! There are lots of footprints here, so we know it wasn't flying.

The bird was standing here. But why? Was it eating the leaves off the tree? Was it waiting for a friend? It wasn't drinking water. The lake's over there!

These footprints are close together. Here, the bird was walking. Those footprints over there are far apart. There, the bird was running.

Look! I can see some birds. But which bird was making these footprints?

**1** Read the story. Which bird made the footprints? Look and mark ✓.

**2** Read and complete the sentences.

a … so we know it _____ flying.

b The bird was _____ here.

c Was it _____ the leaves off the tree?

a emu

b parrot

c cockatoo

23

### Grammar: Past Progressive

We use the past progressive to describe a continuous action or a state in the past.

**Yesterday afternoon, I was playing in the park.**
**We were shopping with Mom on Saturday.**

We form the past progressive with was/wasn't/were/weren't and a verb + ing.

| Affirmative | Negative | Questions | Short Answers |
|---|---|---|---|
| I was walking in the forest. | I wasn't sitting on a flower. | Was he watching TV? | Yes, he was. No, he wasn't. |
| The camels were running through the desert. | The orangutans weren't eating alone. | Were they playing soccer? | Yes, they were. No, they weren't. |

**3) Read and circle the correct word.**

a The emu (**was**) / **were** eating leaves.

b The honeybees **was** / **were** flying over the grasslands.

c The camel **wasn't** / **weren't** running through the rainforest.

d The orangutans **wasn't** / **weren't** sleeping.

**4) Complete with the past progressive.**

a The seal ___was catching___ (✓) fish.
It ___wasn't catching___ (✗) birds. (catch)

b The orangutan _____ (✗) ice cream.
It _____ (✓) fruit and leaves. (eat)

c Some honeybees _____ (✓) over the grasslands.
They _____ (✗) over the city. (fly)

d A polar bear _____ (✓) in the snow.
It _____ (✗) in the forest. (hide)

e The sea turtles _____ (✓) in the ocean.
They _____ (✗) in the swimming pool. (swim)

**Spelling Rule**

play ⟶ play**ing**
dance ⟶ danc**ing**
lie ⟶ ly**ing**
run ⟶ runn**ing**

**5** Look. Write questions and short answers.

a the seal / swim / in the water?
   Was the seal swimming in the water?    No, it wasn't.

b the panda / eat / bamboo?
   _____    _____

c the camels / play / soccer?
   _____    _____

d the polar bears / dance?
   _____    _____

e the orangutan / swing / in the trees?
   _____    _____

**6** Write about what you were doing on the weekend, using the present progressive.

a At 10 o'clock on Saturday morning, I was _____.

b At noon on Saturday, I was _____.

c At 6 o'clock on Saturday evening, I _____.

d At 10 o'clock on Sunday morning, I _____.

e At noon on Sunday, _____.

f At _____.

**Grammar:** Interrupted Past

Hi Sophie,

We're having a fantastic time in Mexico, and we've done some awesome things. When we were visiting the Yucatan Peninsula, my dad and I went on a nighttime walk. We went to a nature reserve where we saw something amazing.

We were walking along the beach when we saw a sea turtle! Sea turtles are endangered, so it was very exciting to see one. We stopped, stayed still, and were very quiet. While we were watching, the sea turtle laid its eggs in the sand. Then, it went back into the sea.

I hope you're having a great summer, too.

Love,

Florence

**1** Read the postcard. Circle the past simple verbs. Underline the past progressive verbs.

**2** Read again and match.

1. When did Florence and her dad go on a nighttime trip?
2. What were Florence and her dad doing when they saw the sea turtle?
3. What did the sea turtle do while Florence and her dad were watching?

a. It laid its eggs in the sand.
b. When they were visiting the Yucatan peninsula.
c. They were walking along the beach.

**Grammar: Interrupted Past**

Two things were happening at the same time:

    **longer action:**    I was dancing.

    **shorter action:**    The music stopped.

We can link the actions in one sentence. We use the **past progressive** to show the longer action, and the **simple past** to show the shorter action.

    I was dancing when the music stopped.

We can link events with *when* and *while*.

    When I was writing a letter, I broke my pencil.
    She fell asleep while she was reading a book.

**3) Circle the correct form.**

a  I **walked** / **(was walking)** in the park when I **(saw)** / **was seeing** my friend.

b  While I **listened** / **was listening** to music, the lights **went** / **were going** out.

c  When I **brushed** / **was brushing** my teeth, I **heard** / **was hearing** a sound.

d  He **ran** / **was running** for the bus when he **fell** / **was falling** down.

e  I **took** / **was taking** pictures when my cell phone **stopped** / **was stopping** working.

**4) Unscramble and make sentences.**

a  playing / when / in the park / started / We were / the storm
   We were playing in the park when the storm started.

b  a fish / was / the seal / swimming / caught / it / While
   _____

c  having / we were / Mom's phone / dinner / when / rang
   _____

d  when / shining / the beach / arrived at / was / The sun / they
   _____

e  my leg / soccer / I was / hurt / playing / when I
   _____

**5** Complete the sentences with the correct form of the verbs.

a  I _was running_ (run) across the street when my friend ___yelled___ (yell) at me.

b  The river _____ (flood) while we _____ (drive) through the town.

c  The orangutan _____ (swing) through the trees when the branch _____ (break).

d  The wind _____ (blow) hard when the tree _____ (fall) down.

e  Juan _____ (talk) on his phone when he _____ (put) his foot in the bucket of water.

**6** Complete the story with the correct form of the verbs.

> swim   see   look   get   ~~happen~~   have   start   fly

Something really funny **1** ___happened___ yesterday while we **2** _____ at the beach.
We **3** _____ a great time when my brother **4** _____ some dark clouds.
We decided to get dressed and go home, but while we were **5** _____ out of the ocean, the wind **6** _____ to blow. When we **7** _____ up at the sky, all of our clothes **8** _____ around!

**7** Write a paragraph about something that happened on your summer vacation.

One day last summer, I _____

_____

_____.

## Improve Your Writing: Possessive Nouns

### Possessive Nouns

Possessive nouns show that something belongs to someone or something.

| Add an apostrophe (')  + s to a singular noun. | Add an apostrophe to a plural noun. | When plural nouns don't end with s, we add an apostrophe + s. |
|---|---|---|

a giraffe's house    the giraffes' house    the women's soccer team

**1** Look. Which phrases are correct? Mark ✓ or ✗.

a   The monkeys' bananas ☐
b   The boys' radio ☐
c   The childrens' teacher ☐

**2** Put the apostrophe in the correct place.

a   Storms are destroying the sea turtles habitat.
b   A sea turtles eggs were on the sand.
c   This sea turtles leg was hurt.

**Writing: A Brochure**

**1 READ** Read the brochure. What's special about Big Tree Wildlife Park?

## Come to Big Tree Wildlife Park
... where you can look into a giraffe's eyes!

**Big Tree Wildlife Park is a wildlife park with a difference: You're always in the trees.**

**What can you do in our treetop village?**
- Move through the trees with the orangutans.
- Have coffee in Marvin the Monkey's Café.
- See Lisa the lion and her cubs from above.

**A few facts about Big Tree Wildlife Park:**
- We opened in 2014.
- We're the only treetop safari park in Western Europe.
- We have over 50 different animals.

**2 EXPLORE** Complete the sentences.

~~pictures~~   imperatives   a list   short

a   _Pictures_ and illustrations make the brochure attractive.
b   We can give lots of information by using _____ .
c   _____ sentences make a brochure easy to read.
d   _____ tell people what to do. They begin with a verb.

**3 PLAN** Think of an interesting place for tourists to visit in your town. What do you know about it? What can you do there? Complete the graphic organizer.

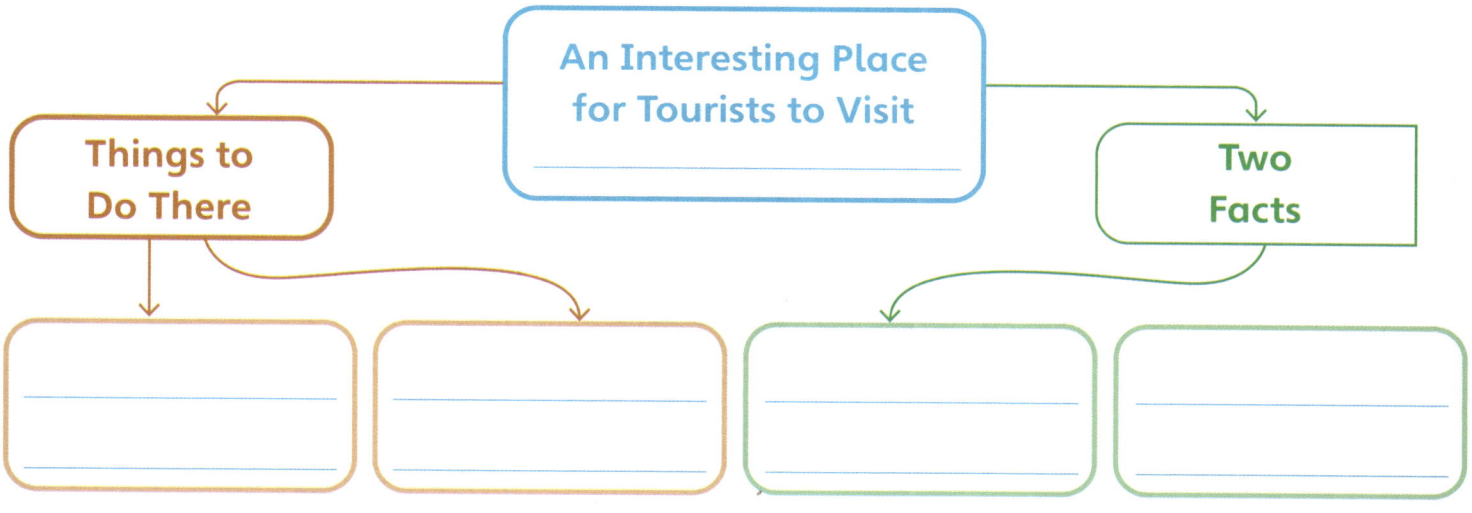

**4 WRITE** Design and write a brochure about the tourist attraction. Use the graphic organizer to help you.

**CHECK**

**Did you ...**
- include lists?
- include illustrations?
- include imperatives?
- use possessive nouns?

# Practice Your Exam Skills

Read the text. Choose the correct words and write them on the lines.

## Orangutans

**Example** Orangutans are a species ____of____ great ape that has red fur.
1 They live in the rainforests of Asia, _____ they spend
2 most of their time high up in _____ trees. The name
3 *orangutan* _____ "person of the forest." Orangutans eat a
4 lot _____ fruit, and they sleep in nests made of branches.
5 Orangutans are very intelligent. At a zoo _____ the United
6 States, the keepers _____ tablets to the orangutans, which they
7 used to play video games. Orangutans _____ an endangered
8 species. Humans are _____ their natural habitat, and there
9 are _____ orangutans living in the wild than in the past.
10 In 100 years, there could _____ no orangutans left.

**Example** from / of / in
1 where / who / that
2 an / the / a
3 mean / means / meant
4 from / at / of
5 on / at / in
6 give / gave / giving
7 am / is / are
8 destroy / destroying / destroyed
9 few / fewer / fewest
10 be / is / are

# 4 What is art?

**Grammar:** Comparative and Superlative Adjectives

## STREET ART

Where do you see art? In a museum? At a gallery? What about outside your house? Some of the best art around can be found on the street.

A street mural is a big picture on a wall or building. Walls with murals are usually brighter and more attractive than walls that aren't painted. 3D murals make you feel like you're stepping into another world.

A lot of graffiti is ugly. It damages buildings and makes people unhappy. However, some people let graffiti artists draw and paint legally. These artists use graffiti styles to make a place look better than before.

Not all artists use paint. Some artists create chalk murals on the sidewalk for people to enjoy. Chalk doesn't last as long as paint, so their murals often disappear after a day.

**1** Read the article. What is it about?

**2** Read the article again. Underline the comparatives and circle the superlatives. Then, complete the sentences with one or two words.

a Some of the ___best___ art around can be found on the street.

b Walls with murals are usually _____ and _____ than walls that aren't painted.

c These artists use graffiti styles to make a place look _____ than before.

d Chalk doesn't last as _____ as paint.

## Grammar: Comparative and Superlative Adjectives

Comparative and superlative adjectives let us compare different things.

**Graffiti is more interesting than paintings.** (Comparative)
**The art museum is the biggest building in town.** (Superlative)

|  | Adjective | Comparative | Superlative |
|---|---|---|---|
| Short adjective (one syllable; some two-syllable adjectives) | The painting is small. | This statue is smaller than the mural. | This is the smallest museum in the world. |
| Long adjective (most two-syllable adjectives; three syllables or more) | It's beautiful. | This flower is more beautiful than that flower. | That building is the most beautiful. |

Some adjectives have irregular forms.
I'm a good artist ⟶ He's a better artist than me. ⟶ She's the best artist.
Jo is a bad cook. ⟶ Sally is a worse cook than Jo. ⟶ Pete is the worst cook.

**Spelling Rule**
tall ⟶ taller ⟶ tallest
nice ⟶ nicer ⟶ nicest
big ⟶ bigger ⟶ biggest
ugly ⟶ uglier ⟶ ugliest

**3 Complete the sentences with the comparative adjectives.**

a Marie has __longer__ hair __than__ me. (long).

b I am a _____ cook _____ my brother. (bad)

c I think playing tennis is _____ watching TV. (healthy)

d Making a sculpture can be _____ drawing a picture. (difficult)

**4 Rewrite the sentences in the correct order.**

a most / That / painting / beautiful / is / the / gallery / the / in
  That is the most beautiful painting in the gallery!

b house / Our / smallest / is / the / the / street / on
  _____

c is / This / nicest / the / shirt / the / in / store
  _____

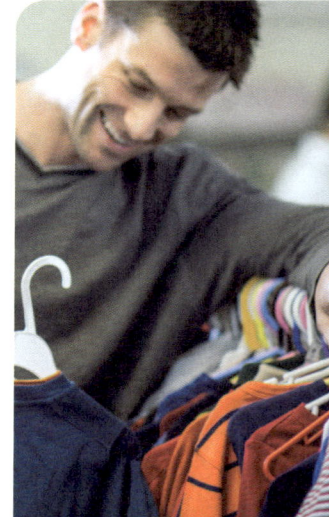

**5** Read the words. Then, write sentences using the comparative or superlative form.

a  red car / expensive / yellow car _____

b  the pink / necklace / long _____

c  Dan's painting / beautiful / Pam's painting _____

**6** Find six mistakes in the message and circle them. Then, write the correct form.

> John? Are you OK? Why weren't you at school?
>
> Hi, Alice. I was at the dentist. My toothache was (badder) this morning.
>
> That's not good. I hope you are gooder now. We had the best time in art today. We learned how to create graffiti art.
>
> But graffiti makes a place look more uglier!
>
> Not if you're an artist. Some graffiti artists are really good. They can make a boring wall look colorfuler. When you look at wall murals, they can make you feel more happier.
>
> That's amazing. I love art.
>
> Well, you should be a street artist. It's easy than you think if you are good at art.

a  _worse_
b  _____
c  _____
d  _____
e  _____
f  _____

**7** Make three sentences about yourself using the comparative or superlative form.

My _____ is _____ than my _____.

My _____ is the _____.

_____

## Grammar: Comparative and Superlative Adverbs

Hi, Claudia!

I won first prize in the art competition last week!

We only had one hour to draw or paint something, so I had to work more quickly than ever before.

Angela, the best artist in the school, was drawing more slowly and carefully than me. She also worked the most quietly, and didn't seem worried at all. She made me feel nervous!

Tony sang loudly as he painted. He sings better than I do, but that still doesn't mean that he's a good singer! I couldn't concentrate at all.

I only had fifteen minutes left, and there was nothing on my canvas. Then, I started throwing balls of colored paint on my canvas. I threw harder and faster each time. My painting was a mess!

However, my classmates thought that, out of the whole class, I had painted the most beautifully.

Take a look. Do you like it?

Pamela

SEND

**1 Read the email. Then, correct the sentences.**

a  Claudia is writing to Pamela.   _Pamela is writing to Claudia._

b  The best singer in the school is Angela.   _____

c  Tony is a good singer.   _____

d  Pamela's painting was neat.   _____

**2 Read the email again and complete the sentences using the comparative or superlative form.**

a  Pamela had to work _____.

b  Angela worked the _____ out of all of us.

c  Tony sings _____ Pamela.

d  Pamela threw the paint _____ and _____ each time.

**Grammar:** Comparative and Superlative Adverbs

Adverbs describe how an action is done. We use comparative and superlative adverbs to describe how one action is done in comparison with other actions. Most comparative and superlative adverbs are made with *more* and *most*.

    **Mike sings loudly.**    Mike sings more loudly than Jill.
                                       Sam sings the most loudly.

Adverbs that have the same form as an adjective have comparatives and superlatives with *–er* and *–est*.

    **Sally runs fast.**    Sarah runs faster than Sally.
                                  Paul runs the fastest.

There are some irregular adverbs, such as *well* and *badly*.

    **Jack dances well.**    Helen dances better than Jack.
                                    Pete dances the best.

    **He draws badly.**    She draws worse than him.
                                 I draw the worst of all.

**3** Complete the chart with the correct form of the adverbs.

| Adverb | Comparative | Superlative |
|---|---|---|
| loudly | more loudly | the most loudly |
| slowly | more slowly | a _____ |
| b _____ | faster | the fastest |
| beautifully | c _____ | the most beautifully |
| carefully | more carefully | d _____ |
| high | e _____ | the highest |

**4** Read and mark ✓ for the correct sentences.

   a  A tiger can jump higher than an elephant.
   b  You should ride your bike more slower in the streets.
   c  John runs fastest than Mike.
   d  Of all her classmates, she dances the most beautifully.
   e  Of all her family, Jane cooks the worst.
   f  Pedro paints more carefully than Paolo.

**5** Read and circle the correct words in each sentence.
   a   Jane should run even **faster** / **fast** to win the race.
   b   The child spoke **softly** / **more softly** than his brother.
   c   Joanne works **more carefully** / **the most carefully** than all the other students.
   d   The dog is barking **more loudly** / **loudly** than he usually does.
   e   Out of all the students in the class, Terry jumped the **higher** / **highest**.

**6** Rewrite the sentences in the affirmative, negative, or question form.

   a   Helen / got up late / Joe.
       ✓ Helen got up later than Joe.
   b   Lucy / spoke angry / of all the people here today.
       ✓ Lucy spoke _____.

   c   the baby played / less noisy / the children.
       ✗ The baby played _____.
   d   Mom / feels good / today than yesterday.
       ❓ Does Mom feel _____?

**7** Write two sentences about different family members using comparative or superlative adverbs.

My sister speaks more softly than my brother.

Out of everyone in my family, my brother draws the most carefully.

## Improve Your Writing: Pronouns

**Pronouns**

Pronouns include *I, you, he, she, it, we,* and *they*. We can use a pronoun to replace the name of a person or thing that we have already mentioned.

John has a new bike. **He** also has a new kite.

The painting was beautiful. **It** won first prize.

Mary and I enjoy watching TV. **We** also enjoy listening to the radio.

We use pronouns when we don't want to write the name again and again.
David is my best friend. ~~David~~ **He** is ten years old. ~~David~~ **He** likes baseball.

**1** Read the sentences and circle who or what the pronoun refers to.

a Penny bought a few new clothes. <u>She</u> also bought a pair of shoes.
(**Penny**) / **clothes**

b The children worked quietly in class. <u>They</u> were good students.
**the class / the children**

c The dog slept under the tree. <u>It</u> snored a little, too.
**the dog / the tree**

d My best friends and I love art lessons. <u>We</u> are good artists.
**my best friends and I / art lessons**

**2** Complete the sentences with the correct pronoun.

a Jill loves taking the dog for a walk. _____She_____ also likes bathing it.

b Ahmed and Andy finished their homework early. _____ also finished their science project early.

c Tanya and I always go for long walks. _____ also play tennis after school.

d You and your sister should help me clean up. _____ should also both clean your rooms.

e The dog loves playing in the backyard. _____ loves to run around and play catch.

**Writing: A Diary Entry**

**1 READ** Read the diary entry. Where did Sarah go?

__c__ Tuesday, May 15

_____ I went to an art studio with my art class today. There were two artists there, and they showed us a few portraits. I couldn't figure out what they were of at first, but I loved the bright colors.

The artists explained that they were abstract portraits. I looked more closely at one portrait and saw a woman in it. It was amazing! _____

Then, one of the artists asked me to sit on a chair in front of her. She also told me to sit still and smile. I sat on the chair and waited.

_____ I felt nervous at first. Then, when I saw that she was painting my portrait, I was so excited! The artist gave me my portrait, and now it's in the living room. It's really colorful, too, and it's beautiful. _____

I think I want to be an artist when I grow up.

**2 EXPLORE** Read and label the following items in the diary entry.
   a   what Sarah did
   b   how she felt or thought
   c   the day and date
   d   descriptive adjectives

**3 PLAN** Think about what you will write about in your own diary. What did you see or do? How did you feel? Complete the graphic organizer.

**When and where?**
_____
_____

**What did you see or do?**
_____
_____

**How did you feel?**
_____

**What did you think?**
_____

**What adjectives can you use?**
_____
_____

**4 WRITE** Write your diary entry. Use the graphic organizer to help you.

_____
_____
_____
_____
_____
_____

**CHECK**

**Did you ...**
- write the day and date? ☐
- write where you went and what you did? ☐
- write how you felt and what you thought? ☐
- use adjectives? ☐
- use pronouns? ☐

**Practice Your Exam Skills**

Look and read. Choose the correct words and write them on the lines.

**Example** This person draws, paints, or makes sculptures. _artist_

paintbrushes    photograph    chalk

| | | |
|---|---|---|
| 1 | This makes a wall or building look brighter and prettier. | _____ |
| 2 | You can go to this place to see paintings and drawings. | _____ |
| 3 | A drawing or painting of a person. | _____ |
| 4 | You use these to paint with. | _____ |
| 5 | Street artists use this to create murals on the sidewalk. | _____ |
| 6 | Material that can be used to make a sculpture. | _____ |
| 7 | The opposite of exciting. | _____ |
| 8 | You can see these in an art gallery. | _____ |
| 9 | Ordinary graffiti that isn't art can look like this. | _____ |
| 10 | Something that is created using a camera. | _____ |

ugly

~~artist~~

works of art

art gallery

portrait

boring    mural    modeling clay

42

# 5 Why do we travel?

**Grammar:** Comparatives

Hi, Lety!

I hope you're well.

We're in the rainforest today. It's fantastic! There are lots of monkeys and gorillas here. The gorillas aren't as funny as the monkeys, but they are less noisy than the monkeys.

Yesterday, we went down the river on a canoe. Our guide showed us a snake. It was as long as our boat!

We go swimming in a river every day. I think it's more relaxing than swimming in the ocean because there are so many beautiful plants.

The gorillas are my favorite thing about the rainforest.

Do you like the postcard?

Tim

**1** Read the email. What is Tim's favorite thing about the rainforest?

   a  the gorillas      b  the museums      c  the beautiful plants

**2** Read and complete the sentences.

   a  The gorillas __aren't__ as funny _____ the monkeys, but they are _____ noisy _____ the monkeys.

   b  Our guide showed us a snake. It was _____ long _____ our boat!

   c  I think swimming in the river is _____ relaxing _____ swimming in the ocean.

**Grammar: Comparatives**

We use comparatives to talk about how things are the same and different. We can use *(not) as … as*, *less … than*, or *more … than*.

  Seeing the shipwreck is **not as exciting as** seeing the turtles.
  A town is **less noisy than** a city.
  The beach is **more relaxing** today **than** yesterday.

**3** Look and complete the sentences using comparatives.

  a  The red car is not _____as new_____ as the blue car. (new)
  b  The new watch is more _____ the old watch. (expensive)
  c  The sleeping bag is less _____ the bed. (comfortable)
  d  The dog is _____ as the cat. (young)

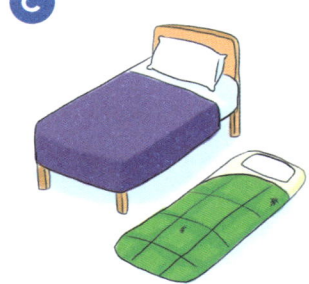

**4** Choose the sentence that has the same meaning as the first sentence(s).

  1  Mary and I are the same height.
      (a) Mary is as tall as me.
       b  Mary isn't as tall as me.

  2  Watching TV is relaxing. Listening to music is relaxing, too.
       a  Watching TV is as relaxing as listening to music.
       b  Listening to music is less relaxing than watching TV.

  3  Playing computer games is exciting. Doing homework isn't exciting.
       a  Playing computer games is less exciting than doing homework.
       b  Playing computer games is more exciting than doing homework.

5) **Unscramble and write sentences.**

a more / than / complicated / Math / is / English
<u>Math is more complicated than English.</u>

b A phone / useful / more / is / than / a pencil
_____

c less / intelligent / than / A frog / a horse / is
_____

d cold / not / is / Autumn / as / as / winter
_____

e Swimming / as / as / exciting / is / riding a bike
_____

6) **Read the fact files and circle the correct words.**

The largest creatures in the ocean are whales, and they are very intelligent, too. However, scientists think that dolphins are as **smarter / smart** as whales.

Ants are very small, but they are also very smart. In fact, they're **very /(more)** intelligent than most other insects.

Lions and tigers both roar very loudly, but a lion's roar is **loud / louder** than a tiger's roar.

Asian elephants are very big, but they aren't as **large / larger** as African elephants.

7) **Compare where you live and where you went on vacation.**

> big   noisy   relaxing   exciting   expensive   comfortable

Where I went on vacation is _____ than where I live. It also is _____ and _____. But it is not as _____.

**Grammar: Gerunds as Subjects and Objects**

# Why is traveling good for you?

**Patrick:** Grandpa, you've been to lots of places, haven't you?

**Grandpa:** Yes, I have. I like visiting different places. It's fun. But I also think it's good for me.

**Patrick:** Why?

**Grandpa:** Meeting different people helps me make friends. Learning languages keeps my brain active. And trying new food means I never get bored eating the same thing.
I also get lots of exercise when I travel. Walking, swimming, and skiing keep me fit and healthy.

**Patrick:** What do you like most about traveling?

**Grandpa:** Let me think. I suppose I appreciate my life here more. And that's why the best thing about traveling is coming home.

**1** Read the conversation. What does Grandpa like most about traveling?

**2** Read the article again and match.

1 I like visiting  
2 Learning languages  
3 Walking, swimming, and skiing

a keeps my brain active.  
b keep me fit and healthy.  
c different places.

**3** Circle all the words ending –*ing* in Activity 2.

**Grammar:** Gerunds as Subjects and Objects

A gerund is a noun made from a verb. Gerunds end in *-ing* and can be the subject or the object of a sentence.

| Subject | Object |
|---|---|
| **Traveling** is good for your health. | I love **relaxing** after a long day. |

Gerunds are often used after the words *like, love, enjoy, hate, don't mind, stop,* and *miss*.

Do you **like walking** on the beach?
I **miss skiing** in the mountains.
I **don't mind watching** old movies.

**4** Read the sentences. Circle the subject gerunds in blue and the object gerunds in green.

a (Dancing) at parties is a lot of fun.
b The lost child stopped crying when he saw his mom.
c Walking in the countryside is good for your health.
d Do you like singing in the shower?
e Talking to new people helps you to make new friends.

**5** Read and circle the correct answers.

a **Swim / (Swimming)** is good exercise for your back.
b Cats don't like **take / taking** baths.
c **Walking / Walk** in the park on a sunny day makes me happy.
d My mom doesn't enjoy **getting up / get up** early every day.

**6** Look at the pictures and make sentences. Use the words in the box.

> wait   do   run   ~~play~~

a John and Tina enjoy ___playing___ in the snow.
b _____ around the park is fun.
c Tony doesn't mind _____ the dishes after dinner.
d I hate _____ for the bus in the cold.

**Read the conversation and complete the sentences using gerunds.**

> Hi, Pedro! Let's go to the pool.

> Hi, Sally. I don't like **1** _swimming_. (swim)

> OK. Then, why don't we go to the park and get some exercise? **2** _____ is good for our health. (run)

> No, thanks. I went to the park in the morning. **3** _____ karaoke is a lot of fun. (sing) Let's do that.

> No, thanks! I can't sing at all.

> Well, there's an action movie on TV tonight. Do you like **4** _____ ? (watch TV)

> Not really. I know! I have a new computer game! Do you want to play that?

> Sure! I love **5** _____ computer games! (play) Let's do that!

**8** **Write four sentences about you or your family and friends using gerunds. Include the words in the box.**

> love   like   enjoy   don't like

My sister likes painting pictures.

_____

_____

_____

48

## Improve Your Writing: *Because*

### Because

We use *because* to give a reason about why things happen or why people feel, think, or do something.

> Many tourists visit Mexico City because it's a beautiful city.
> Many animals are in danger because some people hunt them.
> Billy loves riding his bike because it's fun.

**1 Connect the sentences using *because*.**

a Marie doesn't enjoy computer games. She thinks they're boring.
   *Marie doesn't enjoy computer games because she thinks they're boring.*

b Tess love running. It helps her keep in shape.
   _____

c I like vanilla ice cream. It's delicious.
   _____

d Exercise is good for you. It helps you stay healthy.
   _____

**2 Unscramble and write the sentences.**

a it's a lot of fun / because / I like swimming.
   *I like swimming because it's a lot of fun.*

b because / it rains a lot in rainforests / it is always warm
   _____

c people travel by plane / it's faster / because
   _____

d they help us to stay healthy / because / we eat vegetables
   _____

**Writing: A Travel Blog**

**1 READ** Read the blog about London. Why does Liz think everyone should visit London?

**1** May 2020

**2** City Blogs: Exploring London

There are lots of things you can do in my country's capital city, London.

**Here are three of my favorite things to see and do in London:**

**3** The best way to start your day in London is to visit Hyde Park. Walking or cycling in Hyde Park is very relaxing. At the top of the park is Kensington Palace with its beautiful garden. I think Kensington Palace is the most beautiful palace I've seen.

After visiting Hyde Park, you can take the bus or train to Big Ben, London's famous clock tower. There, you can see the Houses of Parliament and the River Thames next to it.

Lastly, shopping! There are many famous streets in London, but one of the most famous is Oxford Street. I prefer shopping at Camden Market, though, because the market stalls there aren't as expensive as the big stores.

**4** I think everyone should visit London because there are so many things you can see and do there. Write a comment below and tell us what you can do in your own capital city.

**2 EXPLORE** Read again. Find the following items in the blog and write the numbers.

_____ Title

_____ Date

_____ Why everyone should visit London

_____ Three things you can do in London

**3 PLAN** Think about what you will write about in your travel blog. Write the name of the city and what you can do there. Why should people visit? Complete the graphic organizer.

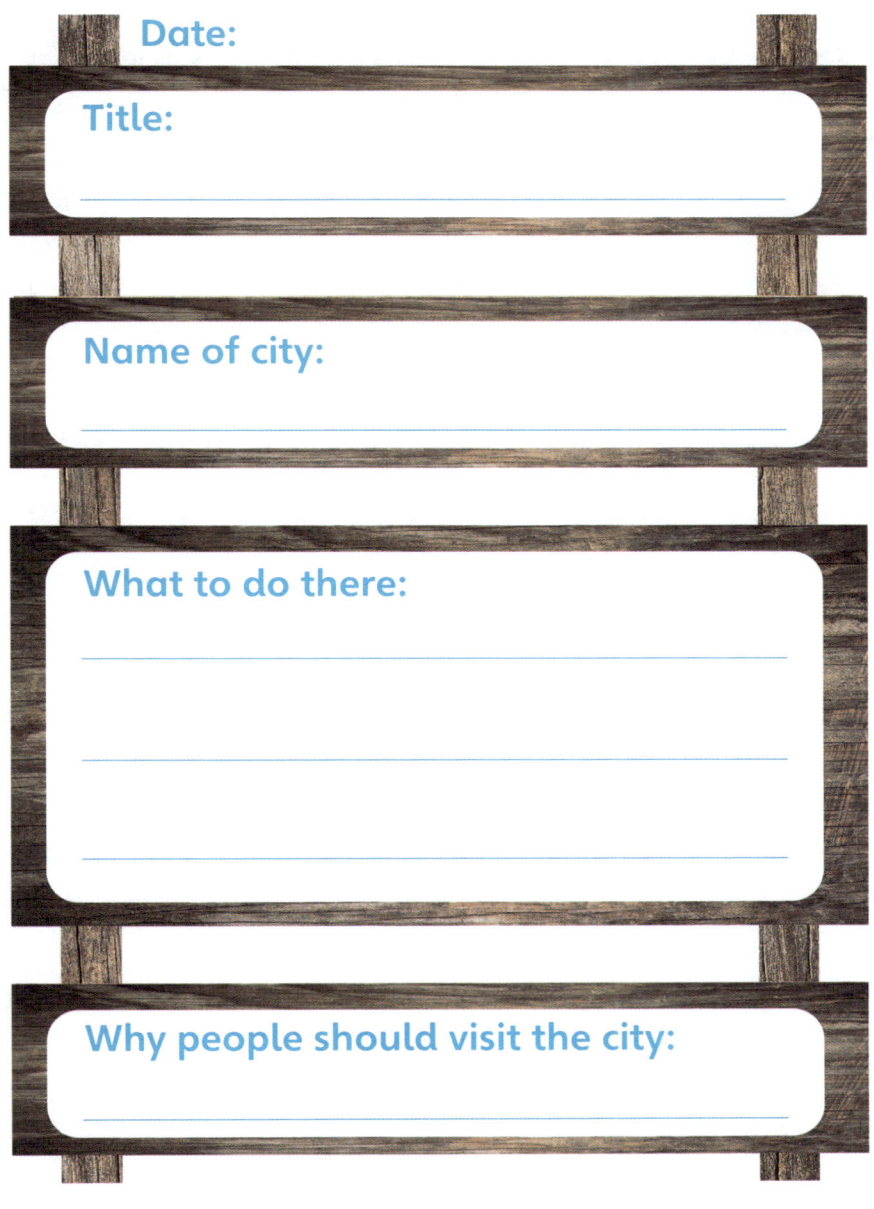

Date:

Title:
_____

Name of city:
_____

What to do there:
_____
_____
_____

Why people should visit the city:
_____

**4 WRITE** Write your blog. Use the graphic organizer to help you.

**CHECK**

Did you …
- include the date? ☐
- include the title? ☐
- give reasons to visit? ☐
- use adjectives? ☐

## Practice Your Exam Skills

1 Read the story. Choose a word from the box. Then, write the correct word next to numbers 1–5.

> ~~vacation~~   tree   cats   boxes   go
> went   cities   villages   because   late

Last week, we went on ___vacation___. We stayed for one week. We didn't stay in the city or even in a hotel. We stayed on a farm!

Every morning, we got up early and helped the farmer with the animals. My dad milked the cows, and my brother and I collected eggs for breakfast. Then, we **1**_____ to the kitchen and helped our mom make breakfast.

After that, we went to the orchards to pick fruit. I picked apples, and my mom picked pears. We put them in big **2**_____, and the farmer sent them to the markets.

We had a small picnic lunch under a big **3**_____ on the farm. Then, we fed the animals. The best part of the day was in the afternoon because we rode horses to the different **4**_____ around the farm. It was a lot of fun!

Dinner was early in the evening, and we all helped to prepare it. We went to bed early because we were all very tired.

We didn't pay the owner of the farm any money **5**_____ we helped him. This type of vacation was more interesting than any other vacation because we learned about farms and taking care of animals.

2 Now choose the best title for the story. Check one box.

Lunch on a Farm ☐     Animals on a City Farm ☐

A Different Type of Vacation ☐

# 6 Why do we play sports?

**Grammar:** Zero Conditional

## UNUSUAL SPORTS

Do you like playing sports? If you don't like regular sports, you can play some very unusual ones!

**Underwater Hockey**
You play this game underwater. You can only touch the puck with a short stick. If you touch a person or the puck with your hands, it's a foul. The team that scores the most goals wins. Teams play another 15 minutes if the game is tied.

**Cycle Ball**
The purpose of this game is to get the ball into the net, not with your feet, but with your bike. Your hands and feet must always be on the bike. If a player touches the floor, they can't play anymore.

**Sepak Takraw**
This is a very popular game in Southeast Asia. It's like volleyball, but you don't use your hands to get the ball over the net—you use your knees, legs, feet, head, or chest. The other team gets a point if you touch the ball with your hands. Teams play another 15 minutes if the game is tied.

**1** Which sentence is correct? Mark ✓.

   a In underwater hockey, you push the puck with your hands. ☐
   b Sepak takraw is similar to volleyball. ☐
   c You can't play cycle ball with your bike. ☐

**2** Read the article again. Then, count how many sentences use the zero conditional. Finally, match the sentences below.

   a If you touch the puck with your hands in underwater hockey,
   b In sepak takraw, if you touch the ball with your feet,
   c In cycle ball, if your hands or feet aren't on the bike,

   1 you don't lose a point.
   2 you can't play.
   3 it's a foul.

> **Grammar: Zero Conditional**
>
> We use the the zero conditional to talk about something that is the result of something else. The zero conditional presents facts and ideas that are generally true.
>
> We use a comma when the sentence starts with *If*.
>
> **If you touch hot water, you burn yourself.**
>
> When the *if* is in the middle of the sentence, we don't use a comma.
>
> **You can get sunburned if you sit in the sun for too long.**

**3  Read and match.**

1  If you eat well,            a  we play boardgames inside.
2  If babies are hungry,       b  you feel good.
3  If it rains,                c  I go to the library.
4  If I have time after school,  d  they cry.

**4  Complete the sentences with *if* + verb.**

a  ____If____ you ____sit____ for too long in the sun, you get sunburned.

b  You feel tired _____ you _____ (not sleep) well at night.

c  We wear warm clothes _____ it _____ (be) cold outside.

d  _____ she goes to the beach, she _____ (wear) a hat.

e  _____ we are in a library, we _____ (not talk) loudly.

5) **Look at the pictures and complete the sentences.**

a. If you heat ice, it _____melts_____ (melt).

b. If you _____ (hold) the ball, the referee blows his whistle.

c. Plants die if you _____ (not give) them water.

d. The team gets a trophy if it _____ (win) the final game.

6) **Put the words in order to complete the sentences using the zero conditional.**

### WATER AND OUR BODIES

1 _If you mix hydrogen and oxygen_ (hydrogen and oxygen / If / you mix), you get water—something we can't live without.

Like plants and other animals, we need water to live.
2 _____ (drink / we / water / don't / If) for more than a week, we die. This is because our bodies need water to work properly. 3 _____ (our / have / bodies / don't / If / water), our blood can't carry food and oxygen to our organs.

If it's hot, 4 _____ (keeps / us / cool / water). This is why we sweat—it's water that comes through our skin from inside our body which helps us stay cool.

If we don't have enough water in our bodies, 5 _____ (our / joints / stiff / feel). This is because water helps our joints move smoothly.

7) **Complete the sentences with your own answers using the zero conditional.**

a. If you finish your homework early, _____.

b. If you study hard, _____.

c. If you eat lots of fruits and vegetables, _____.

**Grammar:** *have to*

# Let's play!

Sports aren't just for fun. Many people play sports as a career. They have to work very hard to be successful.

Alie is a track runner. He has to train before school and after school every day. He has to eat well, and he has to go to bed early.

Lara wants to be a professional tennis player. She normally practices three times a week, but when she has a game, she has to practice more.

Audrey and Jessy are sisters. They both love playing water polo. They don't have to play in big competitions yet because they are still young.

I love running. When I'm older, I want to teach sports. I have to work hard, but I don't mind.

Sometimes I have to practice five days a week. I don't have to go to the gym, though, so that's OK.

One day we want to play in the Olympics. We have to train very hard.

1. Read the text and the speech bubbles. Who wants to play in the Olympics?

2. Read the text again and complete the sentences.

   a  Alie _has to_ to eat well.

   b  Lara _____ practice more before a game, but she _____ go to the gym.

   c  Audrey and Jessy _____ play in big competitions yet.

## Grammar: *have to*

We use *have to* to describe an obligation or something that we need to do. For example, if someone tells us to do something, we use *have to*.

We use *don't have to* when we don't need to do something, but can do it if we want to.

**We don't have to play tennis today.**

The verb after *have to* doesn't change.

**I have to buy some new notebooks.**

**You have to focus in class.**

With *he*, *she*, or *it*, we use *has to* or *doesn't have to*.

**Mika has to eat more healthily.**

**David doesn't have to go to school. It's a vacation day.**

**3 Read and match.**

1 Celise and Yolanda have a big game on Saturday.
2 Kate has a bad cold.
3 Grandpa isn't feeling very well.
4 Mom and Dad are always tired.
5 I cleaned my room yesterday.

a He has to see a doctor.
b They have to get some rest.
c She doesn't have to go to school today.
d I don't have to clean it again today.
e They have to train hard.

**4 Read and circle the correct words in each sentence.**

a Jane **have to** / **has to** train more if she wants to win the race.
b We **doesn't have to** / **don't have to** bring all our books to school today.
c I **has to** / **have to** eat more fruits and vegetables.
d We **has to** / **have to** get more exercise to be healthy.
e Niko **don't have to** / **doesn't have to** wear a coat—it's too warm!

**5** Complete the sentences with the correct form of *have to* or *don't have to*.

a Miguel __doesn't have to__ go to school today. It's Sunday!

b Maddie _____ study harder.

c They _____ run fast to catch the bus.

d We _____ walk to school today.

**6** Write sentences using the correct form of *have to* and *don't have to*.

a Jim / have to / study hard to be doctor
   Jim has to study hard to be a doctor.

b Tina / have to / be nicer / to her sister
   _____

c We / not have to / babysit tonight
   _____

d I / have to / be more careful / when I ride my bike
   _____

**7** Write your own sentences using the correct form of *have to* and *don't have to*.

a I have to _____.

b I have _____.

c I _____.

d I don't have to _____.

e I don't _____.

f I _____.

58

## Improve Your Writing: Sequence Adverbs

**Sequence Adverbs**

We can use sequence adverbs to show the order that things happen in.

**First,** cut up some fruit.

**Second,** put some yogurt in a bowl.

**Third,** put the fruit in the bowl.

**Finally,** enjoy your meal.

**1** Look at the pictures. Then, match and write the sentences.

### A Healthy Sandwich

First,       Second,       Third,       Fourth,       Finally,

_____. _____. _____. _____. _____.

a   wash the vegetables.
b   put lettuce on your sandwich.
c   enjoy your sandwich.
d   spread some mustard on the bread.
e   cut the tomato and put it on the bread.

**Writing:** Instructions

**1 READ** Read the recipe. Is this a fruit or vegetable salad?

## Making a Salad

First, wash a tomato, a cucumber, and an onion. Second, peel and chop the cucumber into small pieces. Third, slice the tomato and onion. Fourth, put the vegetables in a bowl. Fifth, add some olive oil and toss the salad. Finally, enjoy your healthy salad.

**2 EXPLORE** Read and mark ✓ the sentences that are true about a recipe.
a It is written in short sentences that are easy to read and understand.
b It includes lots of tenses and conditionals.
c We can write the instructions in any order we like.
d We write the instructions in order with sequence adverbs.

3 **PLAN** Think about your recipe. What's the first thing you need to do? And the second? How do you finish the recipe? Complete the graphic organizer, adding more steps if necessary.

First, _____

↓

Second, _____

↓

Third, _____

↓

Finally, _____

4 **WRITE** Write your recipe instructions. Use the graphic organizer to help you.

_____
_____
_____
_____
_____
_____
_____
_____

**CHECK**

**Did you …**
- use imperatives? ☐
- use short, simple sentences? ☐
- use sequence adverbs? ☐

## Practice Your Exam Skills

Look at the picture and read the story. Write words to complete the sentences about the story. You can use 1 or more words.

### Jenny's Sports Day

Jenny is an excellent athlete. She took part in the sports day last week. First, she swam in the 100 meter race. She came in third and won a bronze medal. Then, Jenny took part in a cycling race.

After that, Jenny helped her friends get ready for the race. She timed how long it took them to run 100 meters. She also gave them some tips on how to win because track is her best sport.

It was time to start the race. All the runners started running as soon as they heard "Go!" Jenny was in front of all the other runners. She heard her name from the crowd. She looked up. Then, she fell and hurt her leg! All the other runners stopped to help her.

"No!" she said. "Keep running. If you stop now, the race stops, too!" But the other runners didn't listen to her. They helped her get to the doctor.

**Example**
The sports day was ___last week___.

**Questions**
1 Jenny gave her friends _____ on how to win.
2 Jenny's best sport is _____.
3 Jenny fell because she _____ at the crowd.
4 The runners all _____ Jenny.
5 Jenny didn't want the runners to stop because she didn't want the race to _____.

# 7 How can we explore the past?

**Grammar:** *may* and *might*

May 23

I was helping Grandma in the garden when we found a big tin box. Grandma opened it carefully. She was afraid there might be something dangerous in it. Inside the box were another two boxes. We opened them, too. One box had old gold coins inside. They might be worth a lot of money because the date on them said 1821. Inside the other box were pearls and necklaces—lots of them. They may be from a queen who lived here a hundred years ago.

We are going to take them to the museum tomorrow.
We may leave them there because some historians might want to study what we found. They may be able to learn more about our past.

I think I might be a historian when I finish school.

Omar

1. Read the diary entry. How many boxes were there in total? Write. _____

2. Read the article again and match.

   1  The gold coins          a  might be a historian when he finishes school.
   2  The jewelry             b  might be worth a lot of money.
   3  Omar                    c  may be from a queen.

**Grammar:** *may* and *might*

We use *may* and *might* when we don't know something for sure. You can use either word because they have the same meaning. After *may* or *might*, we use a verb. The verb doesn't change.

There might be lots of gold under the sand.
We might become famous.
The secret room may also be full of treasures.
Historians may study the coins and jewelry.

**3** Read and choose the correct word.

a He may **is** / **be** in the library.
b She might **has** / **have** lunch with us.
c They may **study** / **studies** on the weekend.
d Charlie might **call** / **calls** us next week.
e It may **rains** / **rain** this afternoon.

**4** Read and complete the conversations.

may visit    might be    might win

Is Amal here?

No, she isn't. She ___might be___ late because of the rain.

Our cousins called us today.

Yes, I know! They _____ us on Saturday.

Dani is practicing really hard for his match.

Yes, he is! He _____ it!

## 5. Read and match.

1. I don't feel very well.
2. Jenny had a big sandwich after school.
3. Alex loves learning about space.
4. Can you hear that noise?

a. He might be an astronaut one day.
b. It may be the wind.
c. I might see the doctor tomorrow.
d. She might not have dinner tonight.

## 6. Look at the pictures and choose the correct words.

a  It **is** / **might be** a starfish.
b  There **is** / **might be** a boat in the ocean.
c  He **has** / **may have** a lot of money.
d  They **will finish** / **may finish** their homework soon.
e  The children **will find** / **might find** the clue because they can see it on the map.

## 7. Write about what you might do this weekend.

a  I might go _____.

b  I may visit _____.

c  I might _____.

d  I may _____.

e  I _____.

f  _____

**Grammar:** *give, send, take, bring, show*

Hi, Martin!

How are you? I can't wait to see you next Tuesday!

This week, I took my dog to the vet. He was sick and had a fever. He's much better now. I also got my exam grades and showed them to my parents. They were happy, but they said I could do better in history. I don't like history at all. :(

It was Aunt Tammy's birthday yesterday, so I gave her a present—I bought her a book of very old photos from the last century. She loved it.

It's my sister Cassie's birthday next month. Cassie showed me the invitation she's making for her party; she's going to send the invitations to everyone next week. Remember to take her a gift—she really likes books about pirates and buried treasure!

Can't wait to see you!

Sally

SEND

1. Read the note again. Who was the book of old photos for?

2. Read again and make sentences.
   - a  Sally gave — Aunt Tammy — a present.
   - b  Sally took — the dog — to the vet.
   - c  Sally showed — her grades — to her parents.
   - d  Cassie is going to send — the invitations.

**Grammar:** *give, send, take, bring, show*

Objects are nouns or pronouns that follow verbs. The verbs *give, send, take, bring,* and *show* take two different objects.

   I gave some flowers to the teacher.

The *flowers* are the thing that I gave. *Flowers* is the **direct object** of the verb.

The *teacher* is the person I gave the flowers to. *Teacher* is the **indirect object** of the verb.

The order of the objects after a verb can change.

| Verb + direct object + indirect object | Verb + indirect object + direct object |
|---|---|
| We brought the water to him. They sent a present to Jessica. | We brought him the water. They sent Jessica a present. |

**Remember!**
If the indirect object is the second object, we put *to* before it.

   I took the book to Jim.

---

**3** Read. Then, write *a* for Verb + direct object + indirect object or *b* for Verb + indirect object + direct object.

1. My friends gave me a present last week.   _b_
2. Tara showed the letter to her sister.   ____
3. Did you take the books to Juan Carlos?   ____
4. We sent my mom some flowers.   ____
5. Tadeo brought the children some candy.   ____

**4** Read and mark ✓ the correct sentences.

a. My friends gave me a present last week.   ✓
   I sent to my friend a birthday card.   ____

b. She gave her old clothes to her friend.   ____
   She gave to her friend her old clothes.   ____

c. They showed to us their vacation photos.   ____
   They showed us their vacation photos.   ____

d. Terry took the dog to the vet.   ____
   Terry took the dog the vet.   ____

67

5) **Look at the pictures and rewrite the sentences. Change the order of the objects.**

a  She gave the baby a bottle of milk.
   <u>She gave a bottle of milk to the baby</u>

b  She sent the letter to her grandma.
   _____

c  He brought me some groceries.
   _____

d  Paolo showed his new home to us.
   _____

6) **Read the email and complete the sentences using direct and indirect objects.**

Hi Amir,

On Friday, we **1** <u>gave our mom a surprise party</u> (gave / a surprise party / our mom). It was really fun. All her friends were there and lots of our family, too. Cousin Tom from the United States **2** _____ (brought / a hat / Mom) all the way from Texas. Great-aunt Norma was there, too. She **3** _____ (photos / showed / us) of Mom as a baby. Our uncle Barry wasn't there, but he **4** _____ (to us / something / sent) for Mom's party—a cake! We **5** _____ (to Mom / the cake / took) and she looked really happy. She loves cake!

What did you do last week?
Mary

SEND

7) **Write sentences about you or your family and friends using direct and indirect objects.**

<u>My sister gave me a book.</u>

gave
send
brought
show

## Improve Your Writing: Capitalization

**Capitalization**

We use capital letters for titles, for the beginning of new sentences, and for the names of people, nationalities, languages, and months of the year.

**I** think **A**nkara is a beautiful city.
**M**y friend **A**na is from **M**exico.
**C**an you speak **I**talian?
**M**y favorite month is **A**pril because April 8th is my birthday.

**1** Rewrite the sentences with the correct capitalization.

a  hasan is teaching tony how to speak turkish.

   Hasan is teaching Tony how to speak Turkish.

b  I love december because it snows.

   _____

c  are you from spain?

   _____

d  can you speak english well?

   _____

**2** Mark ✓ the sentences that have the correct capitalization. Circle the letters that need capital letters.

a  ⓙoanne and ⓓina are going to ⓢouth America this year.  ☐
b  When do you have French lessons?  ☐
c  I think Chinese is a difficult language to learn.  ☐
d  I don't like august because it's too hot.  ☐
e  jack and tyler are always in trouble.  ☐

**Writing:** A News Report

**1 READ** Read the news report about an interesting find. What did the children find?

# DAILY NEWS
SINCE 1928

## _d_ An Interesting Find Behind the Shelves

___ A beautiful gold mask and a few handwritten letters from the 1920s were found behind a secret passage in the town library yesterday afternoon.

___ Rina Thomas and George Sanchez were looking for a book when they accidentally pressed against a bookcase. It opened and the children discovered a small, dark room where they found a gold mask and some old letters.

___ "We looked at the letters, but couldn't read them because they were in a special code," said Rina. The children phoned George's grandfather, who is a historian.

"A mysterious man arrived in town in the 1920s with a small box. The library was a hotel then. These things must be his," the historian said.

The gold mask and handwritten letters are now in the town museum. Experts think they belong to a royal family, but can't say which one yet.

**2 EXPLORE** Read and label where the following items first appear in the news report.

a  phrases that people said
b  names
c  dates or time words
d  title

**3 PLAN** Think about your news report. Write the title. What was the treasure? Who found it? Where was it? What did they do next? Complete the graphic organizer.

Title:

Name of writer:

What was the treasure?

Who found it?

Where was it?

What did they do?

**4 WRITE** Write your article. Use the graphic organizer to help you.

_____
_____
_____
_____

**CHECK**

**Did you ...**
- include the date? ☐
- include dates or time words? ☐
- include names? ☐
- include phrases that people said? ☐
- use correct capitalization? ☐

71

# Practice Your Exam Skills

**Look at the three pictures. Write about this story. Write 20 or more words.**

# 8 How important is electricity?

**Grammar:** *will*

## WILL ELECTRICITY EVENTUALLY RUN OUT?

We use electricity everywhere—in our homes, schools, on our roads, and to help us have fun. But will the electricity ever run out? And what will we do if it does run out?

Professor Merhi is worried. "Lots of power sources that we use to make electricity will run out soon. There won't be enough oil and coal to make electricity in the future." Professor Thomas, another scientist, isn't worried about the future of electricity.

"Scientists are working on new ways to produce electricity all the time. Electricity will be safer and, more importantly, it will be greener. We will use renewable sources of energy—like the sun, wind, and water—to produce electricity," she said.

1. Read the article. Why is Professor Merhi worried about the future of energy?

2. Read and complete the sentences using the examples of *will* and *won't* in the word box.

> ~~will do~~   won't be   will run out   will use

a. And what ___will___ we ___do___ if it does run out?

b. Lots of power sources that we use to make electricity _____ soon.

c. There _____ enough oil and coal to make electricity in the future.

d. We _____ renewable sources of energy—like the sun, wind, and water—to produce electricity.

**Grammar: will**

We use **will** to talk about the future. We use it to make predictions, say what we intend to do, and state facts.

For statements, we use *will* + verb.

**It will rain later.**   **I will be an astronaut when I'm older.**   **They will go home next week.**

The negative form of *will* is *will not*. We often write this as *won't*.

**Max won't have a late dinner.**

For questions, we use *will* + subject + verb.

**Will he come tomorrow?**

**3  Look and read. Then, write *will* or *won't*.**

a  I'm very tired. I ____will____ go to bed early tonight.

b  She promises she _____ be late again.

c  There _____ be enough time to see you tomorrow. Sorry!

d  _____ Basil paint his room this weekend?

**4  Put the words in order to complete the sentences.**

a  this afternoon / go / to the park / will

The children _____.

b  other sources / there / be / in the future / of energy

Will _____?

c  won't be / many / at the movie theater / people / tonight

There _____.

d  go / you / shopping / tomorrow

Will _____?

**5** **Read and complete the conversation using *will* + verb.**

use    happen (x2)    have (x2)

Hi, Jin. Can I ask you some questions about the future, for my school project?

Sure.

Do you think we **1** ___will have___ forests in the future?

No, we won't because people are cutting the trees down. We **2** _____ forests if we plant more trees.

That's true. What about fossil fuels? What do you think **3** _____ to them?

I think they will run out. I think scientists **4** _____ lightning to produce electricity.

Maybe. You never know what **5** _____ in the future. Thanks for your ideas, Jin.

**6** **Write predictions about the future. Think about:**

where you will be in ten years from now
what energy we will have
how people will travel
what our cities will look like

a  I will _____.

b  We will use _____.

c  People _____.

d  Our cities _____.

## Grammar: Future Plans with *going to*

Hi Diego,

We're going to go to a farm. We aren't going to visit a normal farm with sheep and chickens—it's a solar farm!

So, what are we going to do on the solar farm?

The farmer is going to tell us about how the solar farm works. There are lots of solar panels, and they help the farmer grow lots of plants. We are going to learn all about the plants.

There are also lots of beehives at the solar farm. We're going to see how the bees make honey. Then, we're going to eat the honey. I'm going to enjoy that, but I'm not going to stand too close to the bees. Bee stings hurt!

I think it will be a great day. I can't wait! What are you going to do this weekend?

Emma

SEND

**1** Read the email message and mark ✓ the correct sentences.
   a  Emma is going to a solar farm.
   b  She is going to see different types of animals.
   c  She is going to learn about how bees make honey.

**2** Read the message again and match.
   1  Emma is going to                              a  solar power can produce food.
   2  They are going to eat                         b  go to a farm.
   3  The farmer is going to show them the          c  honey.
   4  They are going to learn how                   d  beehives on the farm.

### Grammar: Future Plans with *going to*

We use *going to* to talk about our plans for the future.

We form *going to* sentences with the correct form of *to be* + *going to* + verb.

| Affirmative | Negative | Questions |
|---|---|---|
| I'm going to see a new movie. | I'm not going to buy a new book. | Am I going to go on vacation? |
| She is going to learn about bees. | She isn't going to be with us. | Is she going to cook for us? |
| We are going to visit a farm. | We aren't going to play tennis. | Are we going to play video games? |

We can also use *going to* make a prediction.
**I think it's going to rain.**

**3** Complete the sentences with the correct form of *be + going to*.

a Joe __is going to get__ home early tomorrow.

b _____ (he / take) any medicine for his cough?

c We _____ (run) out of energy soon.

d _____ (you / help) us clean up the beach?

e They _____ (not / arrive) early.

**4** Make two complete sentences with the prompt using *going to*.

a (She / water / the flowers / not play in the garden)
She's going to water the flowers. She isn't going to play in the garden.

b (He / take a taxi / not walk)
_____

c (They / eat pizza / not eat pasta)
_____

d (She / buy a dress / not buy jeans)
_____

5) **Look and read. Then, complete the sentences using *going to*.**

a   She ___is going to return___ her books. (return)
b   They _____ a solar-powered cart. (build)
c   He _____ the bike. (repair)
d   Sonya and Tess _____ shopping today. (go)
e   Jake _____ the bird. (feed)

6) **Look at the chart and make sentences using *going to*.**

|  | Saturday | Wednesday |
|---|---|---|
| **Rina and Sam** | ✗ play with Manuel<br>✓ visit Grandpa | ✗ clean their rooms<br>✓ watch TV |
| **Martha** | ✗ study for her exams<br>✓ make a cake | ✗ go to bed late<br>✓ study in the library |

a   Rina and Sam aren't going to play with Manuel on Saturday.
b   _____
c   _____
d   _____

7) **Write about your week.**

I'm going to _____ on Monday.

## Improve Your Writing: Time Words

### Time Words

We use time words to add detail to our writing about when things happen. They also make our writing more interesting. Time words can refer to:

- the present (*now, today, this week, this morning*)
- the past (*yesterday, last week, last month*), or
- the future (*tomorrow, next week, next month, next year*).

The days of the week and the months of the year can refer to the past, present, and future.

**I am having lunch** now.

**I rode my bike** yesterday.

**We are going to visit our grandparents** next week.

**They will have a test** on Tuesday morning.

**Julie is going home** next month.

**1** Read the sentences and underline the time words.

a  Tonya will see her cousins <u>on Wednesday</u>.

b  Can you help me clean the kitchen next Saturday?

c  We're playing video games today.

d  We visited many museums last week.

e  Do you want to go to the mall this afternoon?

**2** Read, choose, and circle the correct time words. There are two answers for each sentence.

a  Jasmine and Dalia are going to have a French lesson **next Thursday / yesterday / this afternoon**.

b  Cathy broke her arm **tomorrow / last week / on Monday afternoon**.

c  Do you think we should catch the train **last year / tomorrow / in the morning**?

**Writing:** An Advertisement

**1 READ** Read the advertisement about a tablet. What does it use for energy?

# THE GREEN ENERGY-SAVING TABLET OF TOMORROW

Tired of losing your battery charger? Feel annoyed when you can't find a place to charge your tablet? Well, this tablet is for you! You can recharge it in the sun quickly and safely.

It charges within five minutes when it's sunny and ten minutes if it's cloudy.

**No cords or extra batteries needed. Best of all, it uses renewable energy.**

It is usually $99.99, but for this month only, it's $65.99.

**HURRY! SALE ENDS NEXT WEEK.**

**2 EXPLORE** Read again. Find and label the following items in the article. Then, circle the time words.

a heading
b price
c why the tablet is special
d picture

**3** **PLAN** Think about your advertisement. What is your product? What can it do? Why is it special? How much does it cost? Write a heading. Complete the graphic organizer.

**Heading:**
_____

**Why is it special?**
_____
_____

**How much does it cost?**
_____

**Draw it here:**

**4** **WRITE** Write your advertisement. Use the graphic organizer to help you.

_____
_____
_____
_____
_____
_____
_____

**CHECK**

**Did you …**
- include a heading? ☐
- include time words? ☐
- say why it's special? ☐
- include a price? ☐

**Practice Your Exam Skills**

Read the diary and write the missing words. Write one word on each line.

**Example**
Last week, we _____went_____ to the science museum. It was fun!

**Questions**

1. We learned so _____ things. The best thing we saw in
2. the museum _____ a robot! It could do lots of things. You could put your clothes in its stomach and wash them. As it
3. went around the place, it would vacuum _____ floor. It also
4. answered when you asked _____ questions. The best thing about it is that you use the sun or wind to charge it! I think I'm going to have
5. lots _____ robots in my home!

# 9 Why do we have music?

**Grammar:** Making Promises or Offers with *will*

**Mrs. Bray:** Hello, children. Are you ready for the concert tomorrow? Who will bring the violins?

**Keila:** I'll bring the violins and sheet music in my parents' car.

**Mrs. Bray:** That's great!

**Youssef:** I'll bring the flutes, Mrs. Bray.

**Mrs. Bray:** Thank you, Youssef. I'll buy the card and gift for the conductor. Who will bring the food for the musicians?

**Dina:** I will, Mrs. Bray. I promise I won't forget this time!

**Mrs. Bray:** Great! Now remember … be on time!

1. Read the conversation. What are the children getting ready for?

2. Read again. Count how many promises are made using *will* and write. _____ Then write the names.

   a  __Keila__  will bring the violins and sheet music.
   b  _____ will bring the flutes.
   c  _____ will buy the card and gift for the conductor.
   d  _____ won't forget to bring the food for the musicians.

   Youssef
   ~~Keila~~
   Dina
   Mrs. Bray

**Grammar:** Making Promises or Offers with *will*

We use *will* or *will not* (*won't*) when we promise to do or not do something in the future.

    I **will** put away all my toys.
    We **will not** eat all the cake.

We also use *will* when we offer to do something.

    I **will** bake you a cake.

**Remember!**

The contracted form of *will* is *'ll*.

    She **will** buy the gift. ⟶ She**'ll** buy the gift.

The contracted form of *will not* is *won't*.

    We **will not** be late. ⟶ We **won't** be late.

**3  Read and match.**

1 Molly's birthday party is today.
2 We are late!
3 Ssh! The concert is about to start.
4 Keiko can't find her bus ticket.
5 Do you have my book?

a I left it at home. I'll bring it tomorrow.
b Will you bake a cake?
c I'll help her look for it.
d Don't worry. I'll drive you to school today.
e I know. I won't make any noise.

**4  Complete the sentences. Use the verbs in the box.**

> clean up   do   ~~be~~   be   forget   help

a I'll ___be___ home early.
b We won't _____ anything bad.
c We'll _____ you with the housework.
d I'll _____ my bedroom after this show.
e I won't _____ to do my homework this evening.
f They won't _____ late again.

**5** Write the sentences using *will* or *will not* in their contracted form.

a   I will be ready soon.

   I'll be ready soon.

b   We will not be home early.

   _____

c   I will open the windows.

   _____

d   I will not bring the books tomorrow.

   _____

**6** Unscramble to complete the short dialogues.

a  I can't roller skate.

   I ___will help you learn.___
   (help / learn / you / will)

b  I'm so tired today.

   It's OK, Mom. I _____
   (for a walk / take / the dog / will)

c  I _____
   (dinner / ready / get / will)

   And I _____
   (do / afterward / the dishes / will)

d  The game starts at 4 o'clock.

   Don't worry. _____
   (I / forget / won't)

**7** Write three things you promise to do to be a better student.

a   I will listen to my teacher carefully_____.

b   I won't _____.

c   I _____.

d   I _____.

## Grammar: Past Progressive Parallel Actions with *while*

**Maya:** What a disaster the concert was! While we were practicing, the lights were working. But as soon as we started, they broke.

**Joe:** Yeah! And while we were performing the last song, I was playing all of the wrong notes. So embarrassing.

**Terry:** What can I say? Thanks to the wind, my sheet music was flying all over the stage. I didn't know what to do.

**Maya:** Did you see what happened to Mr. Tomson? While he was fixing the lights, some mice were running around the stage. The cat chased the mice, and knocked over his ladder.

**Terry:** My sisters were so scared that they started crying. Dad says they were crying for about an hour!

**Joe:** Well, it's over now. What a night!

**1** Read the chat message. Mark ✓ for the correct sentence.
   a  The concert was a success. ☐
   b  Maya had a lot of fun. ☐
   c  The performance had many problems. ☐

**2** Read the chat message again and complete the sentences.

   a  The lights were working _____ the children were practicing.

   b  While Joe was performing the last song, _____ all of the wrong notes.

   c  The mice _____ around the stage while Mr. Tomson _____ the lights.

**Grammar:** Past Progressive Parallel Actions with *while*

We use *while* to talk about two things happening at the same time in the past.
**My dad was fixing my bike while I was watching TV.**

We use the past progressive to show that both actions were long actions that were happening at the same time.
**I was doing my homework (from 6 o'clock to 7 o'clock) while my sister was listening to music (from 6 o'clock to 7 o'clock).**

**Remember!**

We form the past progressive with *was* or *were* and a verb + *-ing*
**He was playing the trumpet while they were playing the drums.**

**3** Read the sentences and circle the verbs in the past progressive.

a Alexia (was jumping rope) while Manuel (was skateboarding).

b While the children were sleeping, it was raining outside.

c Ms. Brown was eating a sandwich while her baby was sleeping.

d While we were swimming, our parents were reading their books.

e Dad was singing while he was taking a shower.

**4** Complete the sentences with the verbs in the past progressive.

a My sister ___was making___ (make) a poster while I _____ (draw) a picture.

b We _____ (watch) TV while the dog _____ (eat) its food.

c The students _____ (take) a test while the teacher _____ (read) a book.

d Meni and I _____ (ride) our bikes while the boys _____ (play) soccer.

## 5 Look at the pictures and make sentences.

a  Sally / water the flowers / while / Sam / planting / a tree
   Sally was watering the flowers while Sam was planting a tree.

b  Manal / feed the bird / while / Omar / play / with the dog

c  Mom / set the table / while / Dad cook

d  Tina and Demi / study / while / Mark / listen to music.

## 6 Complete the sentences with your own ideas.

a  She was sitting down while her friends were dancing.
b  Dad was washing the car while Mom _____.
c  I was making a cake while you _____.
d  Perry and Dan were playing basketball while Miguel _____.
e  Dino was laughing while _____.

## 7 Think about your last weekend. What was happening? Write four sentences.

a  I was having a piano lesson while my brother was playing tennis.
b  I was _____ while _____.
c  _____
d  _____

## Improve Your Writing: Conjunctions

### Conjunctions

We use conjunctions to join two parts of a sentence together. Here are two sentences that are similar.

**I like baseball.   I like basketball.**

We can join the sentences together using *and*.

**I like baseball, and I like basketball.**

We can also remove the second *I like*.

**I like baseball and basketball.**

Here are two sentences that show contrasting ideas.

**We enjoy dancing.   We don't like singing.**

We can join the sentences together using *but*.

**We enjoy dancing, but we don't like singing.**

We only use one conjunction to join two ideas.

**1 Rewrite the sentences using the correct conjunction.**

a  Gabriel will play with Luis, **and / (but)** won't play with John.

b  I'll help you now, **and / but** you'll be able to finish it tonight.

c  You can watch TV tonight, **and / but** you shouldn't stay up too late.

d  He walks very slowly, **and / but** he arrives at school on time.

e  I usually listen to classical music **and / but** rock music.

**2 Join the two sentences with *and* or *but*.**

a  We like playing the guitar. We like singing, too.
   *We like playing the guitar and singing.*

b  Miriam enjoys dancing. She doesn't enjoy playing the guitar.
   _____

c  I have a fish. I have a cat, too.
   _____

d  James bought a new computer. He didn't buy a computer game.
   _____

e  They have orange juice for breakfast. They have cereal, too.
   _____

# Writing: A Music Shape Poem

**1 READ** Read the poem. Does the poet like jazz music?

Loud trumpets, small drums.
Big cymbals, blaring horns with lots of pretty hums.
People dancing and humming as they go along,
Singing their favorite song.
Jazz is my kind of music and makes me sing, rap, and have fun.
Jazz makes me want to dance all day, but not in the sun.

**2 EXPLORE** Read the poem again. Then, underline the adjectives, circle the conjunctions, and write the verbs.

_____

_____

**3** Read this poem. What part of speech are the underlined words?

adjective   verb   conjunction

My guitar and I play all day, We sing to melody and to the beat we ªsway. My guitar and I have fun, All day in the ᵇglorious sun. Together we make music all night long We dance ᶜand sing to our favorite song.

a _____

b _____

c _____

## 4 PLAN
Think about your music shape poem. What is it about? How does it make you feel? What instruments can you hear? How do they sound? Complete the graphic organizer.

| What is the poem about? | How does the music make you feel? | How do they sound? | What instruments can you hear? |
|---|---|---|---|
| | | | |

## 5 WRITE
Write your poem. Use the graphic organizer to help you. Remember to draw it in a shape.

**CHECK**

Did you …
- include verbs? ☐
- include adjectives? ☐
- include conjunctions? ☐
- draw it as a shape? ☐

## Practice Your Exam Skills

**Look and read. Choose the correct words and write them on the lines. There is one example.**

**Example** This is what we call many people together at a place.  _____crowd_____

harmonica　　　　　string

crowd　　　　　　　　　　　　　　　　　　　　　　　　　　　　　　clap

1　The sound you make when you put your hands together quickly.　_____

2　This is what we call a person who plays music.　_____

3　A violin is this type of instrument.　_____

4　A flute is this type of instrument.　_____

5　We sing this to help children fall asleep.　_____

voice　　　　　　　　　　　　　　　　　　　　　　　　　　　　　musician

6　What you use when you sing.　_____

7　A drum makes this kind of sound.　_____

8　A place where an audience stands or sits to watch a concert.　_____

lullaby　　　　　　　　　　　　　　　　　　　　　　　　　　　　drumbeat

9　A rectangular instrument that you blow into.　_____

10　A type of symbol used in sheet music.　_____

wind　　　　　　　musical note　　　　　　　auditorium

92

# Review: Units 1–3

**Read the text. Choose the right words and write them in the blanks.**

Dear Uncle Zack,

Last Saturday **0** _was_ was great. My mom, my dad, my brother, and I **1** _____ to a soccer game. It was really exciting. The stadium **2** _____ full of people and colorful flags. When we **3** _____ for our seats, all the people started to sing. And when the teams scored, we **4** _____ hear anything because it was so loud. Mom **5** _____ like noise, so she isn't **6** _____ to the next game. Another exciting thing happened: we saw Harry Cone. He is my favorite player. He **7** _____ in front of us. I didn't **8** _____ him for an autograph. I didn't have my book. I **9** _____ take it everywhere I go. Oh well, we **10** _____ going to another game next week. I'll ask him then.

Lots of love,

Rebecca

| 0  | is           | (was)        | being    |
|----|--------------|--------------|----------|
| 1  | go           | going        | went     |
| 2  | was          | were         | are      |
| 3  | were looking | looked       | look     |
| 4  | can          | could        | couldn't |
| 5  | do           | doesn't      | does     |
| 6  | go           | goes         | going    |
| 7  | was sat      | was sitting  | sits     |
| 8  | ask          | asked        | asking   |
| 9  | should       | was taking   | mustn't  |
| 10 | be           | are          | am       |

# Review: Units 4–6

**Read the text. Choose the right words and write them in the blanks**

**0** _Visiting_ the zoo is great! Last week, my family and I saw one of the **1** _____ cats I've ever seen, a snow leopard. Snow leopards are big cats, though they are not **2** _____ as lions and tigers. In the wild, they live in the mountains of Central and South Asia. They have white fur, which is **3** _____ than other cats' fur. They need it because they **4** _____ stay warm in the cold places where they live. When it's really cold, they also **5** _____ their tails to keep warm.

Snow leopards are hunters. When they **6** _____ high in the mountains, they attack prey from above. They like **7** _____ their prey down the mountainside. It is **8** _____ way to catch their dinner! Snow leopards are endangered, and people should stop hunting them and destroying their habitat. However, the good news is the population is **9** _____ than it was 15 years ago. Scientists estimate that there are now about 9,000 snow leopards in the world. Hopefully, that number will grow **10** _____ now than before.

| | | | |
|---|---|---|---|
| 0 | Visit | Visits | (Visiting) |
| 1 | more beautiful | most beautiful | beautiful |
| 2 | as big | less big | bigger |
| 3 | thick | thicker | more thick |
| 4 | has to | have to | have not |
| 5 | using | use | to use |
| 6 | be | are | will be |
| 7 | chase | will chase | chasing |
| 8 | better | good | the best |
| 9 | large | more large | larger |
| 10 | quick | more quickly | quickly |